# 4

## Public service through the years

# 5

## Ten chan~ firsts during our first 100 years

# 100 years at the heart of the north east

# Go North East: a centenary celebration

**Researched and written by**
Richard Dyter

**Edited by**
Stephen King
at Go North East

**Published by**
Go North East
Publishing.

**Copyright**
© Go North East,
unless otherwise
stated

This book is a celebration of 100 years of serving the people of the north east. Enjoy stories from the buses, as told by employees; discover how buses have been transformed in terms of safety, comfort and efficiency; challenge yourself with trivia quizzes that will test the knowledge of even our longest-serving employees.

Above all, celebrate with us the values of innovation and customer-focus that have enabled our company to survive and thrive ever since our first omnibus service between Chester-le-Street and Low Fell a century ago.

# 100 years at the heart of the north east

# A personal note from Kevin Carr, Managing Director

In 2012 I was proud to take the helm of the company I have worked in for more than 37 years and since then I have worked to ensure that our efforts to deliver excellence and to develop customer and stakeholder relationships are more effective than ever.

Our emphasis remains on improving service, through communications with our customers. Our Twitter and Facebook activities are testament to this – with over 70,000 followers, we are leading the way nationally as well as regionally for customer interactions via social media. Social networking, allied with our live online customer service and continually evolving passenger consultations are helping us move our service forward leaps and bounds.

We have invested £30 million into the business over the last 18 months with 100 new vehicles, equipped with modern day features such as free customer wifi, audio visual next stop announcements and customer power sockets and have opened a brand new £8.5 million state-of-the-art super depot in Gateshead.

Smart and mobile technologies are delivering more convenient and secure bus ticketing. Not only this, they are also creating exciting new opportunities for our customers by integrating and personalising bus ticketing information and putting it into the palms of their hands.

I have been delighted to lead the company through its centenary year. We have celebrated with a number of different events including our investment in 100 new buses; the 5p bus ride on 7th May which ran 100 years to the hour since our very first bus journey; our very own children's book, Tale of the Century; a staff family summer picnic at Beamish; our staff awards night which was held 100 years to the day that our company was formed; and a centenary carol service for our employees and customers at the iconic Angel of the North.

I hope you enjoy reading this book which brings together our services, staff and customers, and how, together, we have played a part in the progress of the north east, a region we're proud to call home.

**Kevin Carr**
**Managing Director**

# 100 years at the heart of the north east

## Stories from the buses, as told by our employees

As you will see from these stories from some of our employees, it really is people that make the wheels on our buses turn - day in, day out. In a whole century of carrying passengers, our drivers have seen many a colourful day. From the vanishing toddler, to the driver who saved a pensioner's life, to the battles against extreme weather – our dedicated drivers have seen it all! We hope you enjoy hearing just a few of the tales from our buses.

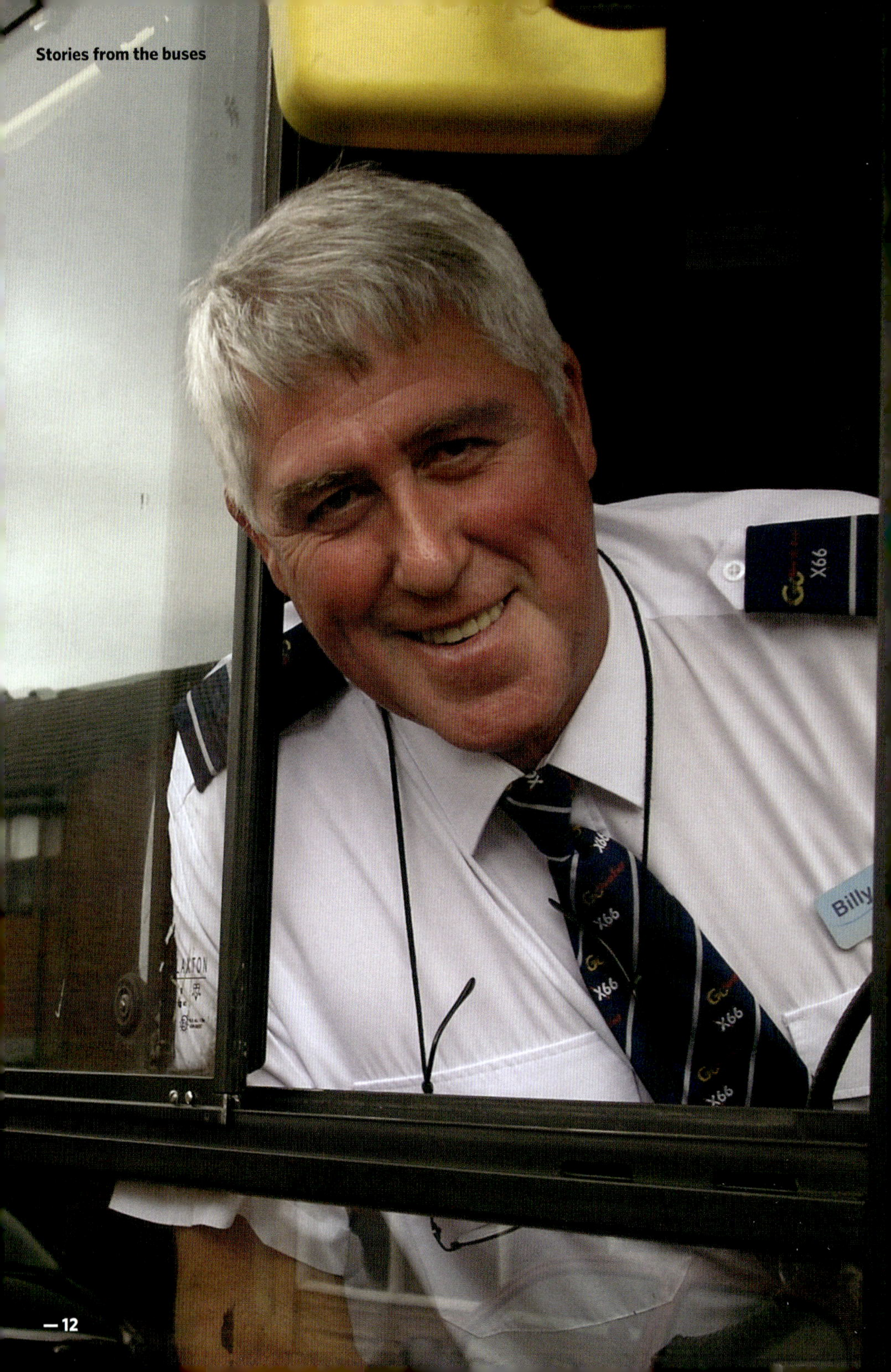
X66
Billy

# A bus service means 'service'

"Buses make our community life richer. We're not just taking people from A to B, we're helping them to live fuller lives – whether it's by taking them to new jobs, to medical appointments, to loved ones or to a much-needed night out on the town.

As part of the service we battle to keep the buses running even when there's ice on the roads, snow in the air and floods across the ground. We want to do the right thing by the people who pay to travel with us and who rely on us to take them where they want to go.

I remember the bitter winter of 1979/80. The gritter lorries were caught up in jams and we were tempted to just halt the buses completely. But we wanted to keep going and to help people get back to the warmth of their homes. The snow was banked up so high that I could only just see the top of the 'bus stop' sign poking out of it. People in some of the villages were cut off for several days. But we got through to them just as soon as we could – with shovels in the back of the bus to dig ourselves out if needed – and we helped them get on with their lives.

In June 2012 there was the most terrific storm – a thunder clap –I've never seen a downpour like it and the floods meant that there were huge jams all along the roads from Newcastle to Sunderland. Most public transport was completely knocked out. Only the buses kept going. I told my passengers: 'We're not going to give up: I'll keep driving this bus no matter how long it takes us. I'm not going to get home until you've all reached your stop.' Eventually I got them all safely to their destination – and I finally finished the longest shift I've ever had to do.

It's amazing how you build up a rapport with your regulars. Every Christmas this lady called Glynis gives tins of Quality Street chocolates for bus employees to share. There are others who like to give us sweets. No wonder some of us drivers can get that little bit larger round the middle!"

BUS
STOP

# Pensioner's life saved by bus driver

"It was this bitterly cold winter's day and there was ice all over the roads. I was going up a steep bank, quite slowly, so I had more time than usual to notice people on the road. There was this pensioner walking a bit unsteadily and it struck me that there was something odd about him.

It took me a few moments to put my finger on what wasn't right. He should have had a thick coat, given the cold weather, but he just wore a thin shirt. And his shoes looked more like slippers than the type of strong shoes you need for an icy day. It looked like he'd just thrown on whatever clothes were at hand, rather than dressing properly for the weather.

The man made me think of my dad, who at that time was suffering from Alzheimer's. So I got on the radio to the depot and asked them to check if there were any missing persons in the area. Sure enough, there was a call out for a man with senile dementia who had wandered out of the back door of his house while his wife was busy in the front room. She was desperate to find him. I told them: 'He's heading up the bank; get the police to pick him up or he'll freeze.'

Sure enough, the police were able to find the chap. They said that if they hadn't reached him when they did, he'd have been dead within the hour as he was already starting to suffer from hypothermia. The man's wife was very grateful but I was just pleased to help – it's all part of us being in the community here."

# Drivers raise money for passenger's family

"There was this lad Kevin who used to travel regularly on the Sunderland bus. He would be there on the same service at the same time most days and all the drivers on that service got to know who he was. He was working as a security guard and one day he got caught up in a robbery at the Co-op Bank in Fawcett Street. He went after the two thieves, using his van to ram their getaway motorbike. He managed to catch hold of one of the thieves and there was a struggle. A sawn-off shotgun was fired at point blank range and Kevin was killed.

It was a real tragedy. Kevin left a young wife and a baby, so it was a desperate situation for them. A group of about 20 of us from the depot got together to raise money for Kevin's family. We did a sponsored bus pull around Sunderland. I can tell you that even with 20 people, and not all of us small people by any means, a bus is a bloomin' heavy thing to pull around. But we did it and we were glad to do our bit for the widow and the bairn."

# Toddler vanishes on bus

"These two women got on my bus, and they were laughing and joking, and they had a pushchair with them. But just as we got towards the next stop, one of them gave this shriek: 'Stop the bus! The bairn's gone! Jimmy's not in the pushchair!'

So I stopped the bus and the mam and her friend looked all over the bus. The other passengers helped as best they could but the toddler had totally vanished. It was a mystery to me: how could the toddler have got out of the bus when we hadn't even got to the next stop?

Whenever you lose anything, the first thing is always to think back to when you last had it. So I asked: 'When did you last see your toddler?'. She made an effort to get herself back together and she thought for a bit. Then she clapped her hand to her forehead and said: 'Oh no! Me and her was so busy chatting and having a tab and all, we've gone and left Jimmy back at Wilkinsons!'

I got on the radio to the police and then I made sure the women got straight back to the store. There, sure enough, safe and sound, was the toddler. So relief all round – not only for the mam and her friend but also for the passengers who'd helped search the bus and who were brilliant that day."

# Every detail helps

"Whenever I drive a bus I'm wearing the company uniform. We're providing a service to the public and appearances matter. That means polished shoes and sticking with the uniform that we've been issued. Mind, we've had a few fashion disasters along the way. Remember the knitted maroon ties of the 1980s? Also, I've been a guinea pig for some uniform ideas that thankfully never made it. Once they tried to make us lady drivers wear really long skirts, which was not practical at all. The uniform we wear today has been tried and tested and I'm happy to look as smart as a driver should.

I think our company is built on people, not buses. Working on the buses is about working with the public. Little things do make a difference, whether it's making sure we make eye contact when passengers pay us their fares or it's helping pensioners to use their bus passes. When I give change to passengers I usually hand it to them rather than just letting it rattle on to the tray. A smile and a greeting help make buses a better experience all round. We try to serve people and we get a lot back from them; it's the passengers that make the job rewarding."

# 100 years at the heart of the north east

## Buses and north east tales

The majority of people from the north east will have heard of the Jarrow March, Sunderland's 1973 FA Cup Victory and The Great North Run. But how many of you know that Go North East played an important role in all these historic events, or how it brought the Blaydon Races to life on the everyday streets of Blaydon? Read on to find out how. It's fascinating stuff.

# Buses and north east tales

# Jarrow March

The Jarrow March of 1936 is one of the iconic events in North East history – and one of our former buses played an important part in it.

It all started during the 1930s when Jarrow was severely affected by the so-called Great Depression. The Palmer's shipbuilding yard was shut down in 1934 and unemployment rose to over 70%, leaving many families struggling to survive and put food on the table. The situation in the North East was one of the worst in the country. With few jobs being created, the town, according to one resident, became a "filthy, dirty, falling down, consumptive area".

The author J.B. Priestley visited the town in the early 1930s and he described the scene in bleak terms: "Wherever we went, there were men hanging about, not scores of them, but hundreds and thousands of them. The whole town looked as if it had entered a penniless bleak Sabbath."

With poor living conditions the mortality rate rose and left the town in a desperate situation. The men wanted to work, they wanted to provide for their families, but this Tyneside town felt unnoticed by the government. It was time to head south and let the Prime Minister know. The plan was to walk down to London, a month-long journey, and take a petition to ask for more jobs.

After medical examinations the 200 fittest men were chosen to take part in the march, alongside Jarrow's MP Ellen Wilkinson who had the nickname 'Red Ellen' because of her left wing politics. As they were going to be on the road for a month, there was a great need for supplies. What would be an appropriate vehicle for transporting all the equipment? What could be better than a bus?

An old SOS PT 4917 bus was bought for £20, which is almost £1,200 today, from one of the Go North East's forerunner companies. The vehicle was loaded with sleeping kits, waterproofs, medical supplies and equipment for hair cutting, shaving and cobbling - not to mention all the food and the cooks.

On 5 October 1936 large crowds gathered and a church service sent off the marchers in style. Even the local children had the day off school to cheer loudly and wave goodbye. With camaraderie and singing, the marching did not seem so bad.

'The 200 fittest men were chosen to take part in the march, alongside Jarrow's MP Ellen Wilkinson who had the nickname 'Red Ellen' because of her left wing politics

**'Today over half a million people use the Crusader bus service to get around'**

The Spirit of Jarrow, sculpted by Graham Ibbeson

However there were many long, cold miles on the open road, plodding through the driving rain. The hills, the mud and the roads took their toll on the shoes and boots, with many wearing out, not to mention the numerous blisters acquired. Cuts, pains and illness were common. Two marchers in particular suffered more serious injuries and were advised that they should go home, but they were determined to stay on and support the marchers. How could they possibly keep up? In the bus of course...

Fortunately there was space on the bus for a couple of passengers. But it wasn't a comfortable journey: the bus was weighed down with cargo and it had to be driven in first gear all the way to London.

The bus had a particularly sticky moment while trying to traverse the steep hills of County Durham. Even with a lot of men pushing hard, the motor could not quite cope. The marchers needed a miracle. What they got was a suggestion to put a teaspoonful of alcohol in each cylinder. Surprisingly that did the trick!

Back on the road the marchers passed through many towns and cities, receiving local support including the offers of halls to hold meetings and places to stay overnight. They picked up more donations from generous onlookers and the petition carried on rapidly growing at each stopover.

The marchers finally reached London on 31 October 1936. There were large public meetings in London where thousands of people turned out and heard speeches from Red Ellen. Surely the Prime Minister had to take notice of them now?

In fact, the Prime Minister refused to see them. All the marchers received was £1 towards the train fare home to the North East.

Still, the marchers' efforts went down in history and they were received back in Jarrow as heroes.

As for the bus, it didn't survive long after its big journey. But its spirit lives on today in Go North East's Crusader route which travels through Jarrow from Newcastle to South Shields. So whenever you travel on our Crusader service, the number 27 between South Shields, Jarrow, Gateshead and Newcastle, take a moment to remember the tradition of the Jarrow marchers.

# Buses and north east tales FA Cup Victory

1973 was certainly a year to remember for one of our bus drivers from the Jarrow Depot. He was driving a double decker Daimler Fleetline bus when he made the mistake of going under a low bridge: scrape...scrunch. The top of the double decker buckled and needed to be cut off and replaced.

Meanwhile, on the football pitch, another close encounter was about to take place. Sunderland were then in the Second Division but they had somehow managed to battle their way to the FA Cup Final, inspired by new manager Bob Stokoe. Their opponents were the mighty Leeds United, a team with ten international players and holders of the Cup.

During the match the heavy rain made conditions very difficult for both teams, but the sodden ground helped to reduce some of Leeds' advantage in terms of talent. Then, after 30 minutes, Sunderland's Ian Porterfield scored a goal to put the underdogs 1-0 ahead.

Leeds were an efficient and well-organised side and they began to pepper the Sunderland goal with shots. But Sunderland's goalkeeper, Jimmy Montgomery, defied the top-ranked team with a string of fine saves.

Mid-way through the second half Leeds managed a close range header, which Montgomery desperately palmed away, straight at the feet of a fearsome Leeds player called Peter Lorimer. Lorimer was only 10 yards away and it seemed that he couldn't miss as he blasted the ball towards the goal. But Montgomery threw himself in the way and somehow diverted the speeding ball on to the underside of the bar. It was clear that it just wasn't Leeds' day.

At the final whistle there was pandemonium as Sunderland celebrated an amazing, unbelievable victory against the odds. A further celebration was immediately planned back home in the north east. The plan was for the team to parade through Sunderland in an open top double decker bus.

Wherever could they find a double decker bus that didn't have a top to it? Was there any possible chance that our company might be able to help out? Yes, funnily enough, we had exactly the bus for them, thanks to the unfortunate encounter with the low bridge. The bus was duly modified and prepared for the great parade, just as we did in 1937.

Around half a million people turned out on to the streets to cheer the team and see the FA Cup held aloft. They could also see our bus, already bright red so it matched the Sunderland colours, decorated fit for champions – and looking perfect without its top!

*Left -* Bob Stokoe Statue outside The Stadium of Light, Sunderland

*Below -* The 1973 FA Cup Winners on their parade

*Bottom left -* The 1937 FA Cup Winners also used a Northern bus

*Bottom -* The match day program

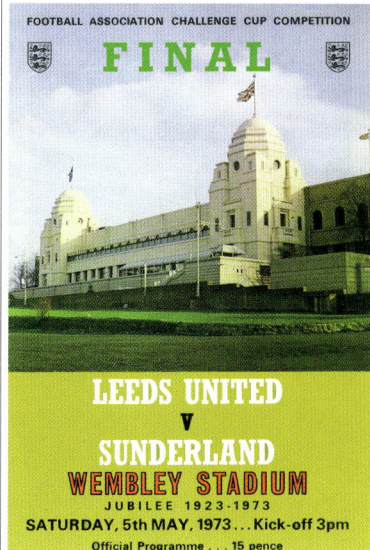

FOOTBALL ASSOCIATION CHALLENGE CUP COMPETITION

**FINAL**

**LEEDS UNITED**
v
**SUNDERLAND**
**WEMBLEY STADIUM**
JUBILEE 1923-1973
SATURDAY, 5th MAY, 1973 . . . Kick-off 3pm
Official Programme . . . 15 pence

# Buses and north east tales Blaydon Races

The 'unofficial' Geordie anthem is the Blaydon Races, a song written by Geordie Ridley in 1862 and later adopted as the marching song of the Northumberland Fusiliers. We've named our number 49 bus service between Winlaton, Blaydon and Gateshead the 'Blaydon Racers' – which is particularly appropriate as the song is all about an eventful journey by bus.

The song describes how the singer takes the omnibus from Balmbra's, which is a pub in the Bigg Market, to go to the horse races at Blaydon. Everyone is in a happy mood as they make their way towards Blaydon, going ('gannin') along the streets of Newcastle.

*"I went to the Blaydon Races,*
*'twas on the ninth of June,*
*Eighteen hundred and sixty*
*two on a summer's afternoon;*
*I took the 'bus from Balmbra's*
*and she was heavily laden,*
*Away we went along Collingwood*
*Street that's on the way to Blaydon"*

*(chorus)*
*Ah me lads, you should*
*have seen us gannin'*
*Passing the folks upon the*
*road just as they were stannin'*
*There's lots of lads and lasses*
*there, all with smiling faces*
*Gannin' along the Scotswood*
*Road to see the Blaydon Races"*

The bus undertakes an eventful journey, with even a wheel coming off the 'bus at one point, before finally arriving at the Blaydon Races. But once there, the passengers find that there are no horses ('cuddy') at the race course because of heavy rain. The only riding that can be done is on fairground horses at a cheap attraction ('a ha'penny roundabout').

*"The rain it rained all day and*
*made the ground quite muddy,*
*Coffy Johnny had a white*
*hat on - they were shouting*
*"Who stole the cuddy."*
*There were spice stalls and monkey*
*shows and old wives selling ciders,*
*And a chap with a ha'penny roundabout*
*shouting "Now, me lads, for riders."*

Next time you're going to Blaydon, hop on the number 49 and enjoy a bus ride that is rather more comfortable and reliable than the journey in 1862 – though you still won't see any horse races as the race course is long gone!

## Revised by Ed Pickford

Local folk singer Ed Pickford changed the lyrics of the famous Geordie anthem in 2012, to reflect his bus journey home on the modern Go North East Blaydon Racers. What do you think? Search for the full version on YouTube.

*"Now I shop doon in Gateshead toon but live up in Winlaton, and when it comes to gannin hyem there's ney hesitation, I gets me sell upon a bus that's caalled the Blaydon Racers, what gans through Swalwell, Dunston, and few meare scenic places."*

# Buses and north east tales | Great North Run

The Great North Run has attracted hundreds of thousands of runners over several decades and we're proud of our role in transporting thousands of runners and spectators throughout the day. This is a massive task, given the huge popularity of the event. There are now 56,000 runners, with participants from over 40 countries, and the Bupa Great North Run is firmly established as the world's greatest half marathon.

When the first Great North Run was held in 1981, plans for the end of the race were not as professional as they are now. Each runner was supposed to have some warm clothes in a plastic bag, ready for wearing after the race. The organisers arranged for some lorries to transport the bags to a series of enclosures near the finish line. The enclosures were numbered in an effort to help runners to find their bag.

In fact, the lorries took the baggage to the finishing area and then, instead of sorting the bags into the enclosures, just dumped them in huge piles. Imagine trying to find your bag among 12,500 of them. It was like looking for a needle in a haystack.

Clearly there needed to be a more reliable approach. In recent years Go North East has been brought into the logistical operation. Part of our role is to provide a fleet of 'baggage buses'. The runners know exactly which bus has their baggage, so they also know which bus to take it from at the end of the race. Problem solved!

These days the Great North Run is organised like a military exercise in order to deliver what's been described as the 'ultimate mass participation running experience'. We love being part of such a lively event that brings so much credit to the north east.

**Left -**
Part of the
Running Suite
series by Peter
Blake, com-
missioned for
the 30th race

**Below -**
The Great
North Run
will see its
millionth
finisher in
2014

**Bottom -**
Our buses
are an integral
part of the
race day
infrastructure

**GREAT NORTH
RUN MILLION**
gnrmillion.org

# 100 years at the heart of the north east

# Public service through the years

Our service has come a long way since 1913. Back in the early days it wasn't uncommon for passengers to get headaches and drivers to vomit out of the window due to being shaken up by the hard tyres that felt every bump in the road. New technology and innovation has massively improved the reliability and comfort of our services – passengers these days need no longer worry about bumpy rides and can even enjoy surfing the internet thanks to onboard wifi.

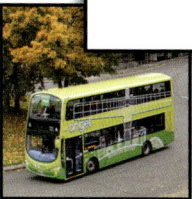

*Above -*
The 604 in its
current state

*Right -*
The 604
during service

# Moving forward with better design

Our company has always stood for innovation and we're proud to have played a key role in the development of the modern bus. In the early years there were two particular issues with how buses were designed, compared to today's situation:

• engines at the front of the bus took up valuable space and reduced the number of passengers that could be carried;

• drivers were stuck in a cab that was some way from the entrance to the bus, making it difficult for them to collect fares when people got on. There always had to be another member of staff – a conductor – to collect fares.

In the 1930s our chief engineer, Mr Hayter, set about producing his own design of vehicle. In 1934 he unveiled a new version of his SE6 (Side-Engined 6-wheeler). This design incorporated two important elements.

Firstly, the engine was under the floor (rather than at the front) so all the floor space in the bus could be given to seats and gangways. Mr Hayter used a special, smaller engine that was imported from the USA.

Secondly, the entrance was in front of the front axle (rather than behind it). For the first time, the driver could control the entrance/exit. This innovation paved the way for what became known as OPO ('One Person Operation') with just a driver and no conductor.

In short, the SE6 can be considered as the first of today's modern buses, which usually have under-floor engines and entrances right at the front of the bus.

The main problem with the SE6 was that it was relatively expensive to build and maintain because it had three axles. Most modern buses have two axles, which means four wheels rather than six, making them cheaper to build and reducing the cost of tyre replacements.

To fix this problem, one of the SE6s – number 604 – was converted to two axles as an experiment. The Government was worried about the safety of a 30-foot bus only having two axles so James Callaghan (later to be a Labour Prime Minister) came to our Bensham depot to check up on no.604. He was duly reassured and in 1950 the regulations were changed to allow buses like the SE6 to operate on two axles.

No.604 therefore has a strong claim to being the most historically important road vehicle ever built in the North East. Its importance meant that it secured a place at the British Transport Museum in 1955. It is currently being restored to its full glory and then it will go to Beamish, the North of England Open Air Museum.

*Above -*
The launch of our brand new depot at Gateshead Riverside, January 2014

*Right -*
A tilt-test of a vehicle before delivery, circa 1964

# More reliable journeys with better vehicles

Back in the early years of our company, buses were not as reliable as they are now. This is hardly surprising; the internal combustion engine was a relatively new invention and powered vehicles were still something of a novelty.

In some ways, the surprise is how infrequently the early buses, for all their mechanical imperfections, did actually break down. In 1913 the company covered 314,283 miles, which is the equivalent of drivingfrom Newcastle to London and back 630 times. That's a lot of miles where something can go wrong.

For the first ten years of our existence most bus services were kept relatively short. This mitigated the consequences of any breakdown and helped ensure that the buses didn't run out of fuel despite their small fuel tanks. Before 1925 it would have been considered downright reckless to take the risk of sending a bus 100 miles from home.

By the 1930s, though, buses were maturing as technology and reliability was markedly improving. This was the era when it became feasible for the first time to consider bus and coach tours as a holiday option. A particularly popular location was Blackpool, at that time one of the ultimate UK seaside attractions.

By the 1980s the company's fleet of vehicles were covering nearly 34,000,000 miles a year. It's the equivalent of 68,000 return trips between Newcastle and London.

By now the reliability was very much better, helped by a wide-ranging service every two weeks as well as a careful schedule of weekly and daily checks.

Today our buses are on a very tight servicing schedule. When a company's reputation rests on keeping services on time, there needs to be a huge focus on eliminating mechanical faults. Each time that a driver takes a bus on the road, he or she has to tick off a whole series of items on a checklist, just like airline pilots.

# Buses for king and country

When war came in 1914 many of our buses were required for the war effort and we gave up half of our fleet of 54 vehicles to the War Office and government work.

In 1939 we again made sacrifices and substantial changes to support the needs of vital wartime industries. We provided hundreds of additional journeys every day to cope with the influx of shipyard workers needed to build more warships and merchant ships.

We also carried no fewer than 14,000 people daily to and from Team Valley Trading Estate, which at the time was one of the largest trading estates in the country. We organised 500 journeys a day and transported about 90% of the workforce. This was on top of 350 journeys a day to the Royal Ordnance Factory at Birtley.

Following Nazi bombing raids on the North East, buses were often needed to cover sections of the railway that had been blown up. The roofs of the buses were repainted grey in order to make them less visible to Nazi aircraft, while the sides were painted olive-green. A sticky netting was applied to bus windows to make the glass more blast-resistant. Headlights were masked in order to avoid attracting attention from the air and interior lights were also dimmed, which made life very difficult for conductors as they struggled to collect tickets. The lack of artificial light made driving very dangerous and more civilians in the region were killed in road accidents than in enemy bombings.

*Left -*
Workers on machine, Ordnance Factory, Elisabethville, Birtley

*Below -*
Workers inside the Ordnance Factory

*Bottom -*
Birtley Volunteers, August 12th, 1914

BIRTLEY MEN WHO VOLUNTEERED FOR THE REGULAR ARMY, AUGUST 12th, 1914.

Gas Bag on Roof Holds Bus Fuel

# Fuelling innovation

In the 1930s the price of diesel was rising sharply and at the same time the coal pits were suffering from lack of demand. Wouldn't it be wonderful if our buses could be converted from expensive imported diesel to north east-produced coal gas?

This idea sounded absolutely brilliant and the company enthusiastically launched trials. The coal gas was stored in bags that were roped to the top of the buses. Coal gas is highly flammable so it was vital to avoid smoking near the bags and generally to protect them from damage. Coal gas is also, by its very nature, lighter than air. In theory a bag could break loose from the top of a bus and drift down to the ground. On one not-so-happy day, the theory became reality.

A driver discovered that one of his gas bags was missing – and it could be anywhere along his route. An act of carelessness by an unsuspecting passer-by could potentially cause a minor fireball and a major accident.

A search was hurriedly mounted and fortunately the errant gas bag was found some miles from Chester-le-Street. No one was hurt and the gas bag was safely recovered. All the same, it was clear that there needed to be a better way to store the coal gas.

A later idea was to compress the gas into cylinders with a pressure of 3,000lb gas per square inch. Unfortunately it was discovered that buses run on coal gas were significantly slower than the usual petro-run buses. The buses also had to keep stopping so that the gas cylinders could be changed, a process that took at least five minutes. Worse, the electricity needed to compress the gas was more expensive than the gas itself. So, with regret, the company had to give up the idea as uneconomic.

Today Go North East continues to invest in alternative fuel options. It currently boasts 18 hybrid electric diesel vehicles in its fleet, operating the iconic Angel route and Sunderland Connect services. Over 40% of its diesel fleet meets the latest Euro 5 and 6 environmental standard, and when combined with those meeting Euro 4 and above gives Go North East one of the cleanest bus fleets in the UK.

Along with colleagues at parent company Go-Ahead, the company continues to explore alternative fuel options such as modern day gas and electric buses and the innovative GKN electric flywheel system, which increases efficiency by using less fuel and therefore reducing carbon emissions. This is based on Formula One race technology developed in the UK.

# Low floor easy access

Arguably, the single most important development in bus design of recent times was introduced to our region in 1994. Along came the truly ground-breaking low floor, easy access bus.

No longer were wheelchair users and parents with pushchairs left out in the cold when it came to bus travel. This clever advancement in vehicle design revolutionised accessibility and we were the first bus company outside of London to adopt it.

The development and introduction of low floor, easy access buses was spearheaded by Chris Moyes, the then commercial director of Go North East parent company The Go-Ahead Group, Tony Kennan from Northumbria Motor Services, who later became chairman of the Disabled Persons Transport Advisory Committee (DPTAC), and Andrew Braddock of London Transport, who were very close friends and former National Bus Company senior management colleagues.

The Dennis Lance SLF (Super Low Floor) Wright Pathfinder bus - registration L469 YVK - was the very first full sized low floor, easy access bus delivered to a provincial bus company in the United Kingdom and was launched in March 1994, under our then Coastline brand. This was followed in October 1994, by a further four vehicles which were used on services 325 and 326 which operated a circular loop around North Shields and Whitley Bay.

We were once again at the forefront of the progression towards bus improvement, just as Northern had been in 1934 with the development of the revolutionary SE6 30' long 44 seat single-decker.

Go North East has continued to lead the way in accessible bus travel with all of our regular services now providing easy access for all passengers through the provision of kneeling low floor and ramp access buses. Our award winning 'Easy Access Guarantee' provides the added reassurance that, should a problem occur, a complimentary taxi will be arranged and our ongoing investment in 'talking bus' technology, means that bus stops are announced and displayed to customers on board.

**Above -**
A scale model produced by Exclusive First Editions

**Far right -**
Our newly produced Accessibilty Guide

Go North East

# Accessibility Guide

Making bus travel easy and accessible for everyone.

Go North East

simplygo.com/**accessibility**

# Embracing social media

Over the last few years we have made the most of a new technology. We have a passion for customer service and innovation, which we firmly believe are responsible for driving growth in passenger volumes and satisfaction levels. This was recognised nationally at the 2012 UK Bus Awards where the company won the prestigious "Putting Passengers First" award.

We were one of the first UK bus companies to have a Facebook and Twitter account and have one of the most integrated social media outputs of any regional bus company in the UK. Our use of social media is genuinely integrated within our customer communications. Positive customer feedback on our effective use of social media is commonplace.

Once the growth of domestic use of social networking facilities was well underway, it was obvious that the business potential in a fast moving public transport environment was significant. We could see that the facility offered the fastest way to communicate operational updates to customers and also the opportunity to promote services, tickets and campaigns using other media. The heavy winter of 2009/10 provided a boost taking the 3000 membership up to 9000. The power of this shift in customer communications was evident - two way, immediate, and informal. We became a dependable friend.

During 2010/11, the growing importance of mobile communication in social networking was addressed through the introduction of a set of mobile apps for Go North East. One to enhance customer communications further, and one which enabled customers to purchase and store their bus tickets on their mobile phone. The apps have received critical acclaim and significant take up.

We have continued the growth of social networking within our customer services team channel mix which was extended to include mail, email, phone and live one-to-one web chat alongside social media. We now receive most of our customer queries via our social media and digital channels.

Today we have 70,000 followers across our social media sites. In 2013, the company was named amongst the 'top 50 travel brands' for social media use in the influential 'Top 100 Brands' compiled by social brand agency Headstream. We were also heralded the 4th most 'socially devoted' company in the UK in an independent report published by social media analysts socialbakers.com which measures organisations on their use of social media and engagement. These results put us alongside big names such as Tesco, British Airways, Argos and Virgin Media. Industry commentators have also acknowledged the progress the company has been making with social media with many transport companies now having their own social media accounts.

# 100 years at the heart of the north east

# Ten changes and firsts during our first 100 years

Needless to say, we have seen a raft of major changes over our first century of running our buses - from shifts in our local industries and communities to great advances in technologies and changes to our environment. Throughout, we have embraced these ups and downs and improved our services for our customers and employees.

Go North East is well known for being at the forefront of innovation. You may be surprised at some of the top ten 'firsts' we can proudly lay claim to.

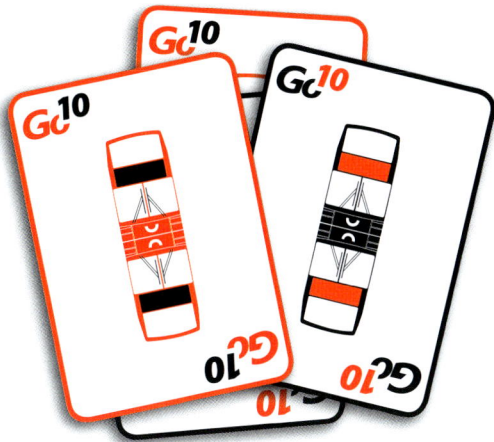

# 1.

## The decline of shipyards and other heavy industries

When the siren signalled the end of the working day, thousands of workers would pour out of shipyards and factories and into rows of waiting buses. The Elswick Works alone employed over 25,000 workers in its heyday. When the last remaining part of the factory closed in 2012 it employed just 600 workers – a decline of 97% in the workforce.

# 2.

## The closure of the coal pits

When we started in 1913, 'King Coal' employed 250,000 men in the north east and the region produced a quarter of Britain's coal. In those days the buses serving the collieries became filled with coal dust; each time you sat down on one of the seats you would send up a puff of black dust. The extinction of the coal industry has been a huge social change.

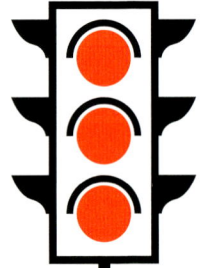

# 3.

## Traffic congestion

One of the biggest headaches when running a reliable bus schedule is the unknown variability of traffic. Cars owned per thousand population has grown by two-thirds since the mid-1980s. However the overall capacity of roads has not grown by a similar proportion.

# 5.

## Passenger habits

During the late 1990s, lots of passengers spoke on their mobile phones. Now there is less talking and more texting and tapping on small screens.

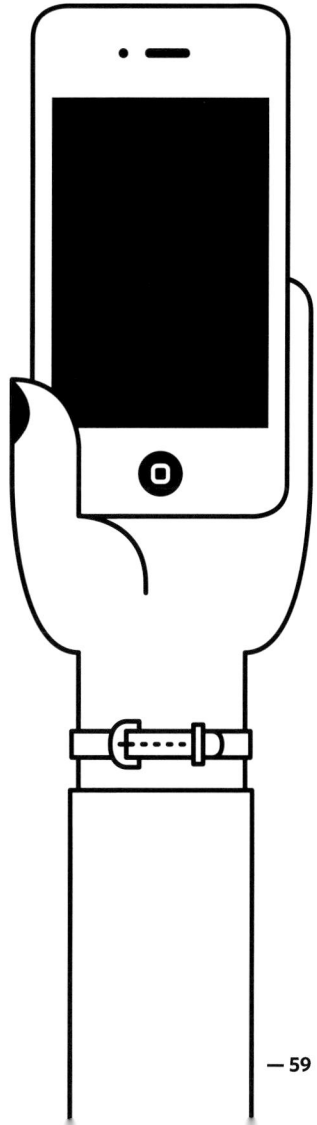

# 4.

## New motorways

A bright spot has been the building of dual carriageways between the major population centres of the north east. Newcastle's Central Motorway opened in 1975.

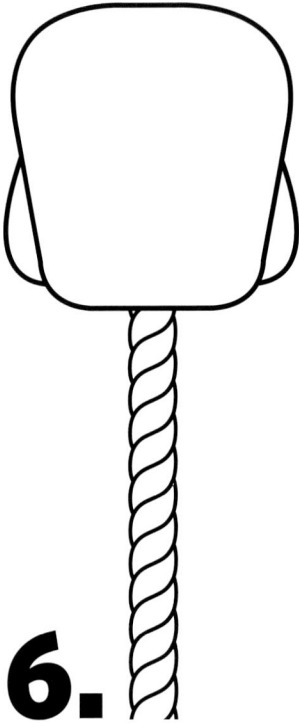

# 7.

## Working with schools

Decades ago, there was no particular help for young people when they moved to secondary school and started to use scholars' buses. But now we work with schools in order to help young people feel confident about bus travel. This smoothens the transition from walking to a nearby primary school to taking a bus to a large secondary school.

# 6.

## Passenger expectations

As bus services become ever better, people's expectations also rise. When we introduced wifi on many services, we also added power sockets for recharging phones, so that passengers' experience is constantly improving.

# 8.

## Smoking ban

The top deck of a bus was where the smokers would congregate to puff away on their cigarettes. When you climbed up to the top deck, it could be like climbing up into a fog. It was most noticeable on the services that took workers home from the factories, as so many people lit up as a habitual part of their end-of-day routine.

# 9.

## Gender balance

In the early days the bus industry was very male dominated. This started to change during World War I when so many men joined the army that women were needed as conductresses. But even in the early 1980s, less than 5% of drivers were female. One of our drivers, Heather Gibbs, started with us in 1981 and she was one of just three female drivers out of 150 drivers at her depot. When she became pregnant, it was considered newsworthy enough for the local paper to come round and interview her.

# 10.

## Branded routes

Traditionally bus companies had a single livery. In the early days our buses were maroon, then in the 1970s many buses were painted either green or poppy red. But what's wrong with a bit of individuality about bus routes? From 2006 we have been 'branding' services with bold eye-catching liveries.

# 1.

## First to cross the Tyne Bridge

The official history of the Tyne Bridge states that it was opened on 10 October 1928 by King George V and Queen Mary, who were the first to use the roadway, travelling in their Ascot landau. But in fact, the first to use the roadway was one of our buses – because the driver wanted to take a sneaky short cut to get back on to schedule. His plan was to nip over the newly completed bridge without anyone noticing. Unfortunately, just as the bus reached the middle of the bridge, the engine spluttered to a stop. The bus was left stranded in full view of everyone. Perhaps just a little embarrassing?

# 2.

## First for extended coach tours in the 1920s

As early as the 1920s we launched extended coach tours, with our first being a seven-day tour to Scotland. An advert in 1938 promised seven-day trips to the 'Cornish Riviera' or 'Glorious Devon' for the bargain sum of £11. However, you were only allowed to take a single suitcase due to space limitations on the coaches. If you had children aged under 12 years, the company generously stated that it might 'consider' a reasonable reduction – but it was up to negotiation.

We also gave people the opportunity of a trip abroad. You could take a plane from Woolsington Airport, now known as Newcastle International Airport, and a luxury coach from our 'continental touring fleet' would meet you at your destination airport. An advert in 1960 claimed that "we have gained the reputation of being 'the' people for Continental Tours in the north east" – and announced the arrival of "truly luxurious" Cavalier 37-seat coaches that are "in advance of anything we have seen yet".

# 3.

## Smoother journeys with comfort tyres

Our first buses had solid tyres, which were widespread among all vehicles a century ago. One of the problems of solid tyres is that they don't absorb any of the unevenness in the road surface.

Passengers used to get jolted, shaken and bumped; sometimes it was worse than being at sea.

We introduced pneumatic tyres on to our buses as early as 1925. This was good news for passengers, who enjoyed a much more comfortable ride.

# 4.

## First outside London to buy brand new Routemasters in the 1950s

The iconic red Routemaster bus was custom-built for London Transport, with its rear-entrance platform suiting the congested streets of London. In the 1950s we ordered 50 of the buses, specially modified to have a larger forward entrance. These were the first Routemasters bought new outside London.

# 5.

## First for award wins

Throughout the years we have won a number of awards that we're very proud of and we remain the most successful company in the region at the various industry awards.

We received the first UK Bus Award for accessibility for our innovative wheelchair guarantee which still stands today. In 2013 we became the first bus operator to win both UK Bus Award Marketing Awards in the same year, sweeping the board!

Our awards over the years mirror the innovations and successful changes to our business such as our route brands, community work, continued investment in staff and services and innovations such as the key smartcard, the mobile ticket and our targeted approach to marketing and communications.

In fact we've won so many awards we have a roll of honour on our website at **simplygo.com/awards.**

# 6.

## First in the north east to be in the top 25 travel 'social brands'

We're one of the top travel companies in the UK for Facebook and Twitter activity. Today we have 70,000 followers across our social media sites. We are amongst the 'top 50 travel brands' for social media use, and are consistently in the top 5 'socially devoted' companies in the UK. For us, it's all part of keeping people informed about the services that they want to use.

# 7.

## First in the north east to operate lower-emission Euro 5 engines

Emissions produced by our buses are among the lowest in the UK. We were the first bus operator in the North East to introduce buses that use the highest standard Euro 5 engines with our Mercedes Red Arrows service. Since then, we have increased the number of buses operating at these standards with our Citylink, Laser, Ten, Silver Arrows and Red Arrows services.

# 9.

## First to win a Green Transport Award for red kite conservation efforts

Red kite birds had been hunted out of existence in the north east 170 years ago. In 2007 a local conservation project, Northern Kites, aimed to reintroduce these graceful birds of prey. We worked with them on numerous projects and set up Red Kite services 45 and 46 between Newcastle and Consett. The buses have frieze panels that carry a wealth of information about the birds and their livery features stunning images of red kites. Our services raise awareness of an important local environmental issue as well as making it easy for people to visit the conservation area. The initiative won the inaugural New Transit Green Marketing Award in 2009.

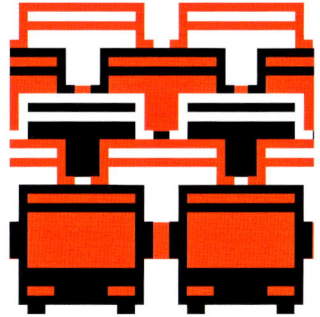

# 8.

## First in the north east to introduce audio-visual announcements

A bus journey can become more stressful if you're going somewhere for the first time and you don't know exactly when you're supposed to get off. Most people have been in that situation: searching for the park on the right, the petrol station on the left, an Indian takeaway ahead...that's when you press the bell apparently. But the windows are steamed up and it's dark outside: help! The good news is that we were the first company in the region to introduce audio-visual announcements of forthcoming bus stops. So you can sit back and relax in the knowledge that the bus itself will tell you where you are now and where you are going next.

# 10.

## First for size in the North East

Go North East is now the largest operator of bus services in north east England, with services throughout Tyne and Wear, Northumberland, County Durham and Teesside. We have a fleet of around 700 buses and coaches that cater for 72 million passenger journeys a year. It's all a long way from that first omnibus journey back in 1913!

# 100 years at the heart of the north east

# Trivia time

Pit your wits against our fun trivia quiz and impress your friends with the fascinating facts in our 'Did you Know' chapter.

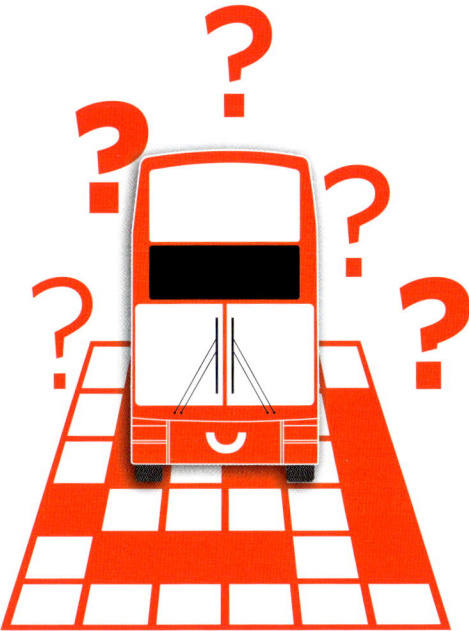

## Question

# 1

**Where does the word 'bus' come from?**

## Question

# 2

**When did the first horse-drawn bus start running in London? Was it 1662, 1789 or 1829?**

## Question

# 3

**What was a charabanc?**

## Question

# 4

**How far can a bus passenger travel for the same fuel consumption per passenger as someone on a short-haul air flight who travels 100 miles? Is it 150 miles, 200 miles, or 250 miles?**

## Question

# 5

**Bus services usually have numbers (such as '66'). Given that there is an infinite supply of numbers, why did bus companies start to use letters as well as numbers (such as '3B')?**

'Bus' comes from the word 'omnibus', which means 'for all' in Latin. The difference between an omnibus and a stagecoach is that no prior booking is necessary – passengers simply get on and get off at any stop of their choice.

The first London 'omnibus' service began in 1829 between Paddington and the Bank of England via City Road.

A charabanc was an early motor coach, usually open-topped. It was especially popular for sight-seeing or works outings. The name comes from the French word for 'carriage with wooden benches'.

For every 100 miles travelled by a passenger on a short-haul air flight, a bus passenger can travel nearly 250 miles for the same amount of fuel per passenger.

Buses have boxes to display the route number. Older buses only had two-track blinds in these boxes so it was impossible for numbers to go above 99. As soon as bus companies started running more than 99 routes (which happened in the 1950s), they had to start using letters as well as numbers.

## Question 6

What word was coined for a female bus conductor?

A female conductor is a 'conductress'. Bus conductors were almost always male until World War I so the word only became commonly used after the outbreak of that war. From the late 1960s there was less need for conductresses/conductors as the drivers were able to collect fares as well as drive the buses. By the 1980s it was only London, with its distinctive Routemaster buses, that still kept two-person crews of driver + conductress/conductor.

## Question 7

When were trams replaced by buses on Tyneside?

In many parts of Tyneside, buses replaced trams in the 1930s. Jarrow tram routes were closed in 1929 and Tynemouth tram routes were closed in 1931. However Gateshead's trams remained until the early 1950s.

## Question 8

Up until 1928, what was the speed limit for 'heavy motor cars'? Was it 30mph, 24 mph or 12 mph?

Until 1928 the speed limit for 'heavy motor cars' was just 12mph. It was then increased to a daring 20mph.

## Question 9

If there are 100 buses in a depot, how many drivers will typically be needed? Is it 100, 200 or 300?

The number of drivers at a depot depends on the number of shifts in operation. Typically there are three shifts, so if there are 100 buses then there will need to be at least 300 full-time equivalent drivers.

## Question 10

Why do some buses have periscopes?

Double decker buses often have periscopes that allow the driver to see what is going on in the top deck. All of our buses now have cctv so that a constant check can be made on what is happening throughout the bus.

# Did you know?

In the 1920s and 1930s it was common for bus drivers on country routes to 'deliver' parcels and newspapers. They did this by throwing them out of the window when they got close to the farm gate or house.

Country buses used to accept livestock as passengers. But one day a goose discovered that its fellow passenger was edible and proceeded to devour it. The company decided it was safer not to work with animals, and banned all livestock.

Our buses in Consett used to be painted cream and yellow but the discharges from Consett Steelworks so discoloured the cream roofs that we had to paint them a darker colour.

Buses used to drive along Northumberland Street, one of Newcastle's main shopping streets, which is now pedestrianised. So did all sorts of other traffic; Northumberland Street was part of the A1 between London and Edinburgh.

Our 1934 commemorative brochure exhorted our staff to "do whatever we can, in whatever small way we can, to keep our bus wheels rolling along smoothly as part of the great industrial machine of the north east".

In the 1940s many QL buses were sold off for £5 as holiday homes. There were whole fields of them near Crimdon on the Durham coast and at Ellington in Northumberland.

Worswick Street bus station was built on such a steep slope that conductors had to put chocks behind wheels to stop the bus rolling away. When it was time to go, the conductors had to grab the chocks and swing themselves on to their bus as it juddered its way out of the station. If the conductors were not very agile, they could easily get left behind.

After World War I there was a shortage of vehicles so the company engineer, Mr Sears, converted some old Army open-backed wagons for service. Passengers risked a soaking if it started to rain so the inventive Mr Sears erected tarpaulins over the wagons, fixed up wooden seats around the sides, and stuck a light in the middle: a 'deluxe effort', according to a report at the time.

One of our early vehicles had interchangeable bodywork, which allowed it to be used as a bus during the week and a mobile fish-and-chip shop at weekends.

**Quiz 2 — Go North East trivia**

## Question 1

What was our first ever bus route in 1913?

a — Low Fell to Chester-le-Street (Number 21 – Angel route)

b — Whitley Bay and Wallsend to Cramlington (Number 17 – Centurion route)

c — Winlaton to Wardley (Number 69 – Pulse route)

d — Newcastle to Gateshead (Number 54 – Saltwell Park route)

## Question 2

Which two of the following bus routes are named after operators that used to operate independently before becoming part of our company?

a — Silver Arrows

b — Venture

c — Diamond

d — Highwayman

## Question 3

We have consistently invested in high quality buses over our 100 years of existence. Which of the following is NOT a type of bus that we have bought?

a — Leyland Atlantean

b — CC-type Daimler

c — Mercedes-Benz Citaro

d — BMW DG522

## Question 4

Depots have always been vital for the smooth running of our bus operations. Which of the following places is NOT a site of one of our depots?

a — Percy Main

b — Beamish

c — Stanley

d — Gateshead

## Question 5

Our buses have been converted for many different purposes. Which one of the following have NONE of our buses been converted to?

**a —**
Operating theatre

**b —**
Mobile library

**c —**
Mobile classroom

**d —**
Mobile fish and chip shop

## Question 6

In the 1920s we provided daytrips for poor children and families to the resorts of South Shields and Whitley Bay. Can you guess the highest number of buses that used to travel in convoy from Consett to the coast?

**a —**
20

**b —**
30

**c —**
40

## Question 7

Shopping centres in the north east generate a large number of bus passengers for Go North East. Which of the following centres was built first?

**a —**
Eldon Square in Newcastle

**b —**
MetroCentre in Gateshead

**c —**
The Bridges in Sunderland

**d —**
The Gates (formerly known as Milburngate) in Durham

## Question 8

Where did we hold our family fun 100th birthday party in 2013?

**a —**
St James Park

**b —**
Stadium of Light

**c —**
Beamish Museum

**d —**
Bowes Museum

— Answers —

1 — a

2 — b and c

3 — d

4 — b

5 — b

6 — c

7 — d

8 — c

— 75

# 100 years at the heart of the north east Acknowledgements

**Go North East would like to thank everyone who contributed to this centenary book, including the many employees who have notched up 20, 30 and even 40 years of service to the company and who generously shared their memories and stories. We would also like to acknowledge the enthusiastic involvement of retired employees and passengers who contacted us in order to contribute to this book, which has been conceived as a people's history rather than as a technical record.**

**Image credits**

All images from the Go North East image library, with the exception of:

**Cover -**
Tom Dodds

**pg 14 -**
Source unknown

**pg 18 -**
Istockphoto.com

**pgs 24 and 27 -**
Superstock.com

**pg 30 -**
Newsprints.co.uk

**pg 33 -**
*Bottom left:*
MirrorPix
*Top and bottom right:*
Courtesy of
Sunderland AFC

**pg 34 -**
Courtesy of
John Coatsworth.
*Image available
to purchase from
Bridekirkfineart.co.uk*

**pg 38 -**
Courtesy of
Great Run

**pg 41 -**
*Top left:*
Peter Blake image
courtesy of Great
North Run Culture.
*Bottom right:*
Tom Dodds

**pg 49 -**
Courtesy of
Gateshead Libraries

**pg 50 -**
Image sourced from
Popular Science
Magazine, Apr 1940

**pg 52 -**
*Top:*
Keith Lee

**pg 59 -**
Courtesy of
Newcastle
City Library

**pg 60 -**
Richard Grantham

**Researched
and written by**
Richard Dyter

**Edited by**
Stephen King
at Go North East

**Further content by**
Jill Farmer

**Design by**
OneNineFour Studio

Every effort has been made to source the rights holders to all imagery in this publication. Please inform us if any errors have been made and they will be rectified in any future editions.